Sherry in the Trifle

A Comedy by Rae Shirley

Evans Plays

London

CAST in order of appearance:

MRS WILL JONES	Aged about 45 she is brisk and business-like, well used to keeping an eye on her husband, Will, and his old dad and not too surprised at what they get up to.
MRS MORGAN	Aged about 70, deaf as a post but couldn't care less, she always seems to hear what she wants to hear and is invariably triumphant with the last word.
BESSIE	Her middle-aged married daughter. She likes having the last word as well - what woman does not?- but, being no match for her mother, fights an eternally losing battle. Unlike MRS JONES, BESSIE only <u>thinks</u> she's the boss where Emlyn's concerned.
CASSIE & CEINWEN LEWIS	Two sisters, minus husbands so far - but they haven't given up hope! Both are of that certain age that is sometimes optimistically described as uncertain.
RACHEL MORRIS	A light-hearted widow with one ambition - not to remain a widow for long!

PRODUCTION NOTES

This play is set approximately six months before THINK THE BEAUTIFUL THOUGHTS - in which both RACHEL and CASSIE are established with regular beaux.

RACHEL, although a regular man-trap, should not be played as a bitchy lady, she's merely on the look out for a likely husband - her third!

CASSIE and CEINWEN (pronounced Kinewen) are both dressed in a fashion that was popular 15 years ago when they were that much younger. They are both trying to delude themselves - and the rest of the world - that they are still bright young things!

BESSIE and MRS JONES are both dressed up to the nines in smart but not necessarily new outfits. BESSIE's new purchase, justified to Emlyn no doubt as being for the wedding, is the Carmen Miranda hat. But it seems unlikely that MRS JONES would waste money on even a hat for Sadie Jenkins' wedding, still less a new outfit!

MRS MORGAN is dressed in her finery - which like CEINWEN and CASSIE can be 15 years old but because she's an old lady it does not look as incongruous as the sisters' outfits.

It is in ortant that RACHEL should be wearing gloves when she first appears so that her engagement ring is not obvious.

For the benefit of the producer, BESSIE's surname is also JONES and if anything can be made of the fact that there are two MRS JONES - do so!

As to the set, the only important thing to remember is that the front door USL should hinge on the DS side and open onto the stage. This will involve everyone except RACHEL in making a quick entrance so that neither they nor their words are shielded from the audience, but it will also mean that there is no danger of the audience seeing whoever is throwing on the hats at the end.

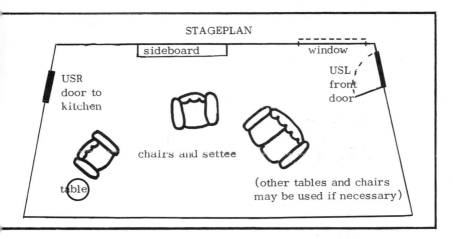

STAGEPLAN

sideboard

window

USL
front
door

USR
door to
kitchen

chairs and settee

(other tables and chairs
may be used if necessary)

table

SHERRY IN THE TRIFLE

Set: The comfortable living-room of MRS WILL JONES. A small
table DR, LC a small settee. USC(L) a window with gaily coloured curtains. Usual chairs, ornaments, TV set etc. Front door USL next to
the window. Door to kitchen USR.
The curtain rises on an empty stage. The front door opens and MRS
JONES enters, followed at a much slower pace by BESSIE and her
mother, MRS MORGAN. They have just come from Sadie Jenkins's
wedding and are all dressed up to the nines with flowers in their
button holes and fancy hats. Of the hats BESSIE's is by far the most
outrageous; reminiscent of Carmen Miranda in her hey-day, it is
smothered in flowers and fruit, a piece of finery completely out of
character with the rest of her - but women are like that about hats!

MRS JONES	(briskly leading the way in) Well, that's over! Come in, come in and make yourselves at home.
MRS MORGAN	(moving stiffly forward on BESSIE's arm and speaking in a high penetrating voice) Beautiful wedding! Beautiful, beautiful! Love weddings, I do.
	(MRS MORGAN and BESSIE both sink gratefully on-to the settee.)
BESSIE	(loosening one shoe slightly) Ooooh, goodness! These new shoes are killing me.
MRS JONES	Hush a minute. Did you hear something out there?
BESSIE	(more engrossed with her feet) No.
MRS JONES	I'm sure there was - (suddenly makes a quick exit UR to kitchen and is heard shouting off stage) Get out, you! Get out of here! Out, out!
BESSIE	(pointing and whispering) New curtains, Mam!
MRS MORGAN	(loudly having smacked BESSIE's hand down) I got eyes in my head, Bessie. I know they're new curtains.
BESSIE	(agonised) Mam, keep your voice down! Oh, I -
MRS MORGAN	(sweeping on) I knew she had new curtains, any-way. Whenever Mrs Jenkins next door has them,

Mrs Jones don't sleep at nights till she goes one better.

BESSIE   Hush, Mam, hush! She'll hear you, I tell you.

MRS JONES   (entering UR) That Will! I told him twice mind to lock the back door, but of course - there it was wide open to the world, with next door's ginger tom pitching into the milk for all he was worth.

BESSIE   Our Emlyn's just the same, isn't he, Mam? You can't trust the men to do anything tidy.

MRS MORGAN   Beautiful wedding! Plenty to eat and drink.

BESSIE   Plenty at that wedding, whatever. None of your one glass ready poured out and lucky to see another!

MRS MORGAN   What was that? Who was lucky?

MRS JONES   (drily) We were! Plenty to eat and drink!

MRS MORGAN   That's what I said, girl. You're getting deaf, the pair of you. (looks around) You got new curtains since I was here last.

MRS JONES   Oh, they're not that new, been up - sure to be a month, at least.

MRS MORGAN   Very nice - if you like colours a bit jazzy-like.

BESSIE   Mam! They're not jazzy-like. They're contemporary - that's what they are.

MRS JONES   It's the very latest. The man in the Co-op said it was straight from Paris.

MRS MORGAN   (stubbornly) I don't care if it's straight from heaven. They still look jazzy-like to me.

BESSIE   Oooh - I got to loosen this shoe a bit more. (takes shoe off completely) Aah! That's better!

MRS MORGAN   Serves you right for shoving a size six into a size four.

BESSIE   I can do what I like with my own feet, can't I?

MRS MORGAN   (giving a gigantic hiccough and patting her chest with gusto) Oh dear! 'Scuse me. It's that raspberry jelly again.

BESSIE	I've told you enough, Mam! (to MRS JONES) Jelly always plays pop with her stomach - but she won't listen.
MRS JONES	(dead serious) Chills her insides up for her, I expect.
BESSIE	That's right. Icecream's the same. She'll suck iced lollies till the cows come home, and me up half the night with her afterwards.
MRS MORGAN	(ecstatically) Ooooh, that ham! I can taste it now. Beautiful, beautiful!
BESSIE	There was real sherry in the trifle, too. Did you have some, Mrs Jones?
MRS JONES	(shortly) I did.
MRS MORGAN	(to BESSIE) What was that you said? Speak up, will you!
BESSIE	(raising voice) Sherry, Mam, in the trifle.
MRS MORGAN	(aghast) No! Sherry in the trifle - and I never had none!
BESSIE	That's your fault. I thought you'd never stop eating that jelly.
MRS MORGAN	(aggrieved) Why didn't you tell me, Bessie? Tch! Sherry in the trifle and I never had none!
MRS JONES	(drily) I believe you!
MRS MORGAN	Duw, it must have cost them a pretty penny. How many were there, do you think?
MRS JONES	They SAID they'd sent out 150 invites, but it did didn't look that much to me.
MRS MORGAN	That's just what I said, Mrs Jones. Two hundred if there was one.
BESSIE	(resignedly) Trust Mam to get hold of the wrong end of the stick. Ah well, Sadie's off their hands now. That's the main thing, I suppose.
MRS MORGAN	What's that you said?
BESSIE	(impatiently raising voice) Sadie's off their hands - and a Good Thing Too!

MRS MORGAN	No need to yell at me. I'm not deaf. When is your Beryl going to name the day, Mrs Jones?
MRS JONES	It won't be long now. I've got an endowment coming out on her father next year.
MRS MORGAN	(condescendingly) She's courting an English fellow, isn't she?
MRS JONES	(on the defensive) That's right, Mrs Morgan.
MRS MORGAN	Never mind, girl. Some of them make good husbands, even if they are English.
BESSIE	(changing the subject) I wonder how much longer the men are going to be?
MRS JONES	If you mean our Will and his father - they'll be there to the bitter end.
MRS MORGAN	Bitter is right!
BESSIE	(smugly) I sent our Emlyn home to see to the fire.
MRS JONES	You're lucky! I dropped the hint to our Will, but nothing doing.
BESSIE	Emlyn tried to act dull, too, but I was up to him.
MRS JONES	What about a nice cup of tea? I know I could do with one.
BESSIE	Oh, thank you very much, Mrs Jones.
MRS JONES	I put the kettle on when I went after that cat. (taking off her hat) Better mind my bit of best, I suppose.
MRS MORGAN	Do you like our Bessie's new hat, Mrs Jones? Special for the wedding she bought it.
BESSIE	(adjusting the hat proudly) A real bargain it was. The girl in the shop said it took years off my age.
MRS MORGAN	What d'you think of it? She looks like a harvest festival, don't she?
BESSIE	(protesting) Mam!
MRS MORGAN	(sweeping on) A bunch of bananas on top of that lot and they'd be giving out the next hymn.

BESSIE	(anguished eyes heavenwards) Oooooooh!
MRS JONES	Well, if we're going to have that cup of tea..... I won't be a moment. (exit UR)
BESSIE	(stage whisper) She's in a mood, she is – what with Sadie Jenkins having such a posh wedding – and before her Beryl, too.
MRS MORGAN	What's that? Who's in a mood? Why should any- one –
BESSIE	(interrupting) Mam, shut up, will you! I wish to goodness you'd wear your deaf-aid. I got a sore throat already.
MRS MORGAN	Why should I? I can hear all I want to hear, if only people would take the trouble to speak up.
BESSIE	Strikes me you only hear what you want to hear.
MRS MORGAN	And why not, I say? It's nice to be able to pick and choose.
BESSIE	Did you see Cassie and Ceinwen at the wedding?
MRS MORGAN	Who?
BESSIE	Cassie Lewis and her sister.
	(MRS JONES enters from kitchen UR apron on and carrying a tray set with cups, saucers, milk, sugar, teapot, biscuits etc.)
MRS JONES	Here we are. That didn't take long, did it?
MRS MORGAN	A cuppa tea, you can't beat it. You know, I'm not right in the morning till I have one.
BESSIE	(eyes heavenwards) And then you're not always right!
MRS MORGAN	(sharply) What was that?
BESSIE	Nothing, Mam. I was just saying, Mrs Jones, did you see Cassie and Ceinwen there?
MRS JONES	(busy with tea-things) See them? The way they were togged up I thought it was them who was getting married!
BESSIE	At their age, too! Talk about mutton dressed up as lamb!

MRS JONES	New Zealand mutton at that!
MRS MORGAN	What's that you said, Bessie?
BESSIE	Cassie and Ceinwen, Mam - mutton dressed up as lamb.
MRS MORGAN	To hear you talk you'd think they were ninety. Why, I was in school with their mother.
BESSIE	And I was in school with them - and I'm thirty-nine.
	(MRS MORGAN starts at this but MRS JONES, having been pouring out the tea, chooses this moment to hand the cups round.)
	Oh, thank you, Mrs Jones. Mam, take your tea, will you.
MRS MORGAN	(to MRS JONES) How old did she say she was?
MRS JONES	(tactfully) I didn't hear, Mrs Morgan.
MRS MORGAN	Well, I did! And you're not thirty-nine, my girl. You're forty-four ..... forty-five next birthday.
BESSIE	(reproachfully) Oh, Mam!
MRS MORGAN	I don't know why you won't admit it. I'm seventy-two and I don't care who knows it.
BESSIE	Oooh, I wish she'd mind her own business.
MRS MORGAN	And I heard that, too. And if my own daughter's birthday isn't my business, I'd like to know what is!
BESSIE	All right, Mam, all right. Point taken, you're right - (under her breath) as usual!
MRS JONES	Like a bit of cake or a biscuit, Mrs Morgan?
MRS MORGAN	Lovely cuppa tea. (as MRS JONES proffers a plate of biscuits) Oh, no thank you, bach. If I ate another crumb, I'd bust my roll-on.
MRS JONES	What about you, Bessie?
BESSIE	Not for me, Mrs Jones, thank you all the same. I'm full to the eyebrows.
MRS MORGAN	A real picture Sadie Jenkins looked in her wedding dress, didn't she?

SHERRY IN THE TRIFLE

MRS JONES	(tartly) Very nice! Pity she was three inches taller than the bridegroom. He looked like a jockey on a diet!
MRS MORGAN	What was that? What did she say?
BESSIE	(raising voice impatiently) The bridegroom, Mam. He looked like a jockey on a diet.
MRS MORGAN	(flabbergasted) Whatever are you on about? Sadie never married a jockey! Wherever did you get that idea from? Jockey, indeed.
BESSIE	(shouting in exasperation) Mam! She only said he looked like a jockey. She never said he was one!
MRS MORGAN	(to MRS JONES) I dunno why that girl will keep shouting at me. Jockey, indeed! What's his name now?
MRS JONES	Whose name?
MRS MORGAN	That chap Sadie went and married.
MRS JONES	Oh, him. Solomon Pugh.
MRS MORGAN	That's it – Solomon Pugh. Yes, I remember the day he was christened. The minister didn't quite fancy the name. Said it was asking for trouble.
BESSIE	What did he mean – asking for trouble?
MRS MORGAN	I don't know, girl, unless he meant all those wives Solomon in the Bible had. Ran into hundreds, didn't they?
MRS JONES	H'mph! This Solomon won't run into hundreds. Sadie Jenkins will see to that.
BESSIE	Fancy her getting married already, and her only leaving grammar school a couple of years ago. Getting younger and younger they are.
MRS JONES	You said it! They're no sooner out of a pram than they're pushing one!
BESSIE	Oh dear! I'm feeling a bit funny. I don't know whether it's my stomach or my head.
MRS MORGAN	(to MRS JONES) What's she muttering about now?

MRS JONES	(raising voice) She's feeling funny. She doesn't know if it's her stomach or her head.
MRS MORGAN	Doesn't know? Don't be so dull, girl! Your head's up there and your stomach's down –
BESSIE	(interrupting) Mam! I know where my stomach is!
MRS MORGAN	I should think so, too. I never heard such a thing. I mean to say, once you start forgetting where your –
BESSIE	MAM! Be quiet, will you! (to MRS JONES) I think I sort of mixed my drinks.
MRS JONES	Silly thing to do that, very silly. What did you have?
BESSIE	Um .... I had pop first .... then port ... and then more pop again.
MRS MORGAN	Who's going pop?
BESSIE	You will in a minute.......! Oh, yes, and there was that sherry in the trifle, too. No wonder I feel funny.
MRS JONES	Lucky to be feeling anything by the sound of it.
MRS MORGAN	(ecstatically) There's a beautiful speech Mr Jenkins made. Fair brought tears to my eyes, it did.
MRS JONES	(tartly) I was nearly crying, too. Thought he'd never stop!
MRS MORGAN	(giving it all she's got) When he said, 'We are not losing a daughter but gaining a son.....' Ooooh! Beautiful! Beautiful!
BESSIE	(patting her chest as she gives a not insignificant burp) Ooh! That's better.... pardon me.
MRS MORGAN	(sharply) What was that? What was that noise?
MRS JONES	(determinedly tactful) Nothing, Mrs Morgan.
MRS MORGAN	Nothing? I could have sworn I heard a dog barking.
MRS JONES	(shortly) We haven't got a dog.

MRS MORGAN	All right, girl, all right. There's no need to go for me. We had a lovely dog once. Pure pedigree he was. Nero we called him - till we had to change it to Nancy. Funny the mistakes people make, isn't it?
MRS JONES	(unsmiling) Very funny. I wonder where that Will is.
BESSIE	(patting her chest again) Oh, that's better.... Stuck right here it was, but it's gone now.
MRS MORGAN	Gone? What's gone?
MRS JONES	Bessie's indigestion.
MRS MORGAN	Oh, there's a pity. I don't like losing things, do you? Much rather give them away.
BESSIE	Oh, Duw..... there's times I wish I could give her away!
MRS JONES	Would anyone like another cup of tea?
BESSIE	No, thanks. I'm right now. Better try and get this blessed shoe on again. Mam, it's time we were off.
MRS MORGAN	You go, if you like. I'm not half ready yet. Any more tea there, Mrs Jones?
	(In silence MRS JONES takes cup and refills it.)
BESSIE	No good to argue with her when she's in this mood. Stubborn as a mule she is.
MRS MORGAN	(chattily) I didn't think old Mrs Elias was looking too well.
BESSIE	Her old man made up for her, with a vengeance. Full of the joys of spring he was.
MRS MORGAN	What was he full of?
BESSIE	(exasperated, shouting) THE JOYS OF SPRING, MAM, THE JOYS OF SPRING!
MRS MORGAN	The way that girl shouts at me you'd think I was deaf, indeed to God you would!
MRS JONES	(drily) Aye! You would!
	(Knock on front door.)

MRS JONES	(going UCL to answer it) Now I wonder who that is .....

(She opens the door. Standing on the doorstep are CASSIE and CEINWEN, two middle-aged sisters, dressed in a desperate attempt to delude themselves and the world that time has stood still for them. Unhappily time has marched relentlessly on - it always does.)

.... Oh, hello Cassie. Ceinwen. Come on in!

CEINWEN	(entering) We thought we'd just drop in for a minute -
CASSIE	(following) - seeing as we were passing, like.
MRS JONES	Sit down, sit down.
CASSIE & CEINWEN	(together) Hello, Mrs Morgan. Hello Bessie.
MRS MORGAN	Hello girls - what did you think of the wedding? Wasn't it beautiful?
CASSIE & CEINWEN	(together) Beautiful!
MRS MORGAN	Yes, indeed. Beautiful!
MRS JONES	(eyes heavenwards) Duw, if we don't know that by now, we ought to!
MRS MORGAN	Love weddings, I do. Plenty to eat and drink!
BESSIE	That's right enough, too. Talk about champagne and cav-arr-ie!
MRS MORGAN	Did you have some of that sherry with the trifle in it?
CASSIE & CEINWEN	(together) Oh, yes, Mrs Morgan.
MRS MORGAN	(much put out) Everybody had some except me! I wish you'd told me, Bessie. She never tells me anything.

(MRS JONES hands CASSIE and CEINWEN cups of tea.)

MRS JONES	Sugar, Ceinwen?

CEINWEN   Oh, no thank you, Mrs Jones. My figure, you
                  know.

CASSIE   Me neither, Mrs Jones. I've got to watch my
                  middle-age spread or it'll be all over the place.

MRS MORGAN   What's all over the place?

BESSIE   Her middle-age spread, Mam.

CASSIE   (bridling) Well, I wouldn't say it was quite all
                  over the place, Bessie. What I believe in is a
                  good foundation garment, don't you?

MRS MORGAN   What does she believe in?

BESSIE   (loudly) Corsets!

MRS MORGAN   (astounded) Believes in corsets? Well, there's
                  a daft thing to say. Believes in corsets! What-
                  ever will she come out with next!

BESSIE   (to CASSIE) Don't take any notice of her, for
                  goodness' sake. She's only showing off because
                  there's company.

CEINWEN   (changing the subject) I like your hat, Bessie.
                  I saw one on television last night just like it.

BESSIE   (delighted) Did you now!

CEINWEN   Hat of the year they called it.

MRS MORGAN   Which year?

BESSIE   (ignoring her) Fancy that, on television you say.
                  (preening herself in her handbag mirror) I must
                  say, I always get plenty of looks when I wear it.

MRS MORGAN   Plenty of what?

BESSIE   (raising voice) LOOKS, Mam. When I wear this
                  hat.

MRS MORGAN   Not a bit of wonder! A blind man couldn't miss
                  it. Talking about a walking allotment!

BESSIE   Mam!

MRS MORGAN   Makes me feel like my dinner every time I see it.

CEINWEN   (wistfully) There's beautiful dress Sadie Jenkins
                  had. Made my mouth water, it did.

CASSIE	Mine, too.
BESSIE	You saw Rachel Morris there, I suppose?
CEINWEN	(grimly) We saw her!
MRS JONES	She's not going to stay a widow for long, the way she dresses. I heard she spent every penny of her first's insurance money on new dresses and now it looks as if Willie's insurance is going the same way.
MRS MORGAN	And why not, I say! If I was as young as Rachel I'd have done the same thing when my old man went.
BESSIE	Now, Mam, don't go getting any ideas. I got enough trouble with Emlyn, without you having to get married again.
MRS JONES	Is it right that Rachel and Silas Ebenezer are courting regular?
MRS MORGAN	Who's courting?
BESSIE	Rachel and Silas Ebenezer, Mam.
MRS MORGAN	You were too slow, Ceinwen. What did you want to let Silas get away for?
MRS JONES	You should have made up your mind when you had the chance.
CEINWEN	You must be joking! I made up my mind - it was Silas.
BESSIE	Oh.....?
CEINWEN	He kept saying he didn't believe in rushing things. Considering we'd been walking out eight and a half years, I wouldn't exactly call that a stampede, would you?
BESSIE	No indeed. I tell you straight, if it hadn't have been for leap year, our Emlyn would have got away. Leap year and Mam, of course.
MRS JONES	You two come straight from the reception now?
CEINWEN	Well, I had to go home first. I laddered my stockings. First time for me to put them on, too.
CASSIE	Ceinwen's always laddering her stockings - and

the price they are today, too. She's only got to
look at them and right away – a ladder!

MRS MORGAN   Who fell down a ladder?

BESSIE   (sotto voce) I wish you would!

CASSIE   It was Ceinwen's –

MRS MORGAN   (interupting) Ceinwen? Serves her right for
going up one!

MRS JONES   Were there many left – at the reception, I mean?

CEINWEN   Only the men. You know what they are!

MRS JONES   (grimly) Aye! We know!

CASSIE   It was getting a bit noisy, so we thought it was
time to go.

BESSIE   Always the same. Once the minister turns his
back they start letting their hair down.

MRS JONES   I bet our Will and his father were smack in the
middle of it.

CASSIE   I never knew Mr Jones had such a nice voice,
Mrs Jones. Singing beautiful, he was.

MRS JONES   (grimly) Was he, indeed! And his old Dad with
him, I suppose?

CASSIE   That's right. Lovely song – 'Only a Rose I Give
Thee'.

MRS JONES   'Only a Rose'! He'll have more than a rose
when he sees me! Never should have left him
there, I shouldn't.

CEINWEN   Quite a duet it was – most of the time.

MRS JONES   What d'you mean – most of the time?

CEINWEN   Well, one was sort-of chasing the other – if you
know what I mean – specially when they started
on the hymns.

MRS JONES   Huh! It was 'Bread of Heaven', I suppose?

CEINWEN   That's right, Mrs Jones. However did you guess?

MRS JONES   It's always 'Bread of Heaven' when they've had
a couple. Wait till I see them! I'll 'Bread of

Heaven' them!

MRS MORGAN	What's the matter now? She's not short of bread, is she?
BESSIE	Men! They're all the same, every man Jack of 'em! You can't trust them out of your sight for a minute.
MRS JONES	You can say that again.
BESSIE	(smugly) Thank goodness I sent our Emlyn home to see to the fire.
CASSIE	(equally smug) It didn't take him long, whatever!
BESSIE	Didn't take him long? What d'you mean?
CASSIE	He came back to look for you - so he said.
BESSIE	Look for me? He hasn't looked for me since the day we were married - and I wouldn't bet on it then! (rising angrily) And me thinking he was safe at home!
MRS MORGAN	Where are you off to now? (to the others) You'd never believe how restless she is. Off, off, off all the blessed time.
BESSIE	I'm going out after that Emlyn.
MRS MORGAN	Emlyn? What's he been and done now, then?
BESSIE	That's what I'm going to find out. Come on, Mam.
MRS MORGAN	(ignoring her) Beautiful speech Mr Jenkins made. Brought a lump to my throat, it did.
BESSIE	Lump in her throat! I'd like to -
MRS MORGAN	(sweeping on) Mind you, I got to admit I ate a bit too much of that jelly but it's passed off now.
BESSIE	MAM!!! I'm waiting for you.
MRS MORGAN	(ignoring her) Fancy old Jim Edwards managing to get there. Never thought he'd ever get out of bed after that last dose he had.
MRS JONES	Yes, he must be eighty-eight if he's a day.
BESSIE	MAM!!!
MRS MORGAN	I'm coming, I'm coming! These youngsters!

Can't stop still a minute!

CASSIE	Like they say in the pictures – 'Ants in their Pants'.
MRS MORGAN	Ants in their where, Cassie?
CASSIE	Pants, Mrs Morgan, PANTS!
MRS MORGAN	(thoughtfully) Oh! Very awkward that would be, wouldn't it?
BESSIE	Ma-a-am!
MRS MORGAN	Hark at her! She's going to do herself a mischief if she's not careful. (slowly gets out of the chair) Well, it's been lovely seeing you all again. Give me your arm then, Bessie girl.

(BESSIE thankfully gives her an arm and MRS JONES gets up to escort them to the door USL.)

Beautiful wedding, beautiful. Love weddings I do. Tch! That's that jelly again......

CASSIE & CEINWEN	(together) So long, Mrs Morgan. Bye, Bessie.
MRS JONES	So long, now.

(BESSIE and MRS MORGAN exit USL. MRS JONES shuts the door after them.)

CEINWEN	She's lasting well, is old Mrs Morgan. Tougher than an old army boot she is.
CASSIE	That's a fact. According to her, she's been seventy-two for the past five years.
MRS JONES	Oh, I don't blame her – forgetting her birthdays. We all do a bit of that, don't we?
CASSIE	(reluctantly) We-ell, yes, I suppose we do ... in a way ....
CEINWEN	I wouldn't care how old I was so long as I was married.
MRS JONES	That's what you think!

(There is the noise of the back door opening and shutting from the kitchen off R.)

RACHEL	(off USR) Anybody at home?

(MRS JONES, CASSIE and CEINWEN exchange significant glances.)

MRS JONES   Rachel.

CASSIE &
CEINWEN   (together) We know!

MRS JONES   (going to kitchen door USR) Come on in, Rachel.

RACHEL   (entering, not at first noticing the sisters) Oh, Mrs Jones, there's news I've got to tell you. (as she sees them) Oh! You've got company.

MRS JONES   Only Cassie and Ceinwen.

CASSIE &
CEINWEN   (together - coldly) Hello, Rachel.

RACHEL   (smiling) Hello, girls. How's tricks!

CASSIE   We saw you at the wedding.

CEINWEN   With Silas Ebenezer.

RACHEL   You don't mind, do you?

CEINWEN   Mind? Why the - why should I mind?

CASSIE   She wouldn't have Silas now if he was to go down on his bended knees to her.

RACHEL   (cheerfully) Oh well, not to worry, girls! He's not likely to do that.

MRS JONES   Like a cup of tea, Rachel?

RACHEL   I don't mind if I do, Mrs Jones.

MRS JONES   I won't be a minute.

             (Exit MRS JONES to kitchen USR taking teapot and empty cups with her. There is a strained silence.)

RACHEL   Er - beautiful wedding, wasn't it?

CASSIE   Beautiful!

CEINWEN   Yes, indeed. Beautiful.

             (Pause.)

RACHEL   Good job it kept fine for her.

CASSIE   Yes. Lucky is the bride the sun shines on, they say.

CEINWEN	(wistfully) Lucky is the bride, I say! Who cares about the sun! (pause as she remembers what she wants to ask RACHEL) Didn't I see you at the pictures last night, Rachel?
RACHEL	I don't know, did you?
CEINWEN	(pointedly) In the back row.
RACHEL	Now, Ceinwen, I may be a widow but I'm a respectable widow – and if there's one place I wouldn't be seen dead in, it's the back row of the pictures.
CEINWEN	(stubbornly) Then if it wasn't you it was your spitting image.
RACHEL	How are you so sure, Ceinwen? Were you there?
CEINWEN	(indignantly) Well! If I never was to move from here I've ....
MRS JONES	(entering from kitchen USR with tea cups on tray) Here we are .... a nice fresh cup.
CASSIE	Mrs Jones, you've never gone and made some more tea for us! Think of my figure!
MRS JONES	(handing round cups) Come on, girl, it's only tea.
RACHEL	Thank you very much. (puts cup down near her) Better take my gloves off. Oh, yes .... I may as well tell you the news first as last. (she brandishes her left hand on which is an outsize diamond ring) Like it?
MRS JONES	(admiringly) Like it? Smashing, girl. You want sun glasses to look at that.
CEINWEN	Oh, got yourself a new ring?
RACHEL	Got myself an engagement ring.
CASSIE & CEINWEN	(together) ENGAGEMENT RING!
MRS JONES	Use your eyes, girls. Can't you see what finger it's on?
CEINWEN	(sharply) Who to?

RACHEL	(archly) I give you three guesses.
CASSIE	(mournfully) I don't need three guesses.
MRS JONES	Silas Ebenezer, of course.
CEINWEN	(shattered) Not him .... not Silas Ebenezer!
RACHEL	And why not? We've been walking out getting on for six months now.
CEINWEN	Six months ..... six months? What the – what's six months? Eight and a half years he was courting me!
RACHEL	I know, Ceinwen, but you never got a ring out of him, did you?
CEINWEN	And to think I gave him the best years of my life.
RACHEL	(not unkindly) Well, I'm sorry, love. Just the luck of the draw, as my first used to say. Mind you, Silas is very fond of you. He told me so himself.
CEINWEN	So he ought to be. Kept him in suppers for years I did – not to mention tea on Sundays.
CASSIE	And don't forget the Welsh cakes he used to take home for his mother.
RACHEL	He always says he feels like a brother to you, Ceinwen.
CEINWEN	Thank you all the same, Rachel, but I've got a brother.
MRS JONES	When's the wedding to be, Rachel?
RACHEL	In the spring. It won't be a white wedding, of course, with me a widow twice over but there'll be an invite for all of you, I promise.
CEINWEN	(getting up with dignity) Thank you all the same, Rachel, but that's one wedding I shan't be going to. Coming, Cassie?
CASSIE	Me, neither. (gets up) So long, Mrs Jones.
MRS JONES	I'll come to the gate with you.
CEINWEN	(opening front USL) No need. So long, both.

RACHEL

So long.

(CEINWEN and CASSIE exit USL shutting the door behind them.)

MRS JONES

Poor old Ceinwen - and Cassie, too. Pity for them, mind. They'd have made good wives for somebody.

RACHEL

They've had as much chance as I've had - and Silas will be my third.

MRS JONES

Nice little business he's got. He must be worth a tidy bit.

RACHEL

Well, he's not exactly another Richard Burton, is he? If he wasn't worth something - well, I won't say I'd have said a downright 'no' - but I'd have taken a damn sight longer to say 'yes'.

MRS JONES

He's not as young as all that to be getting married for the first time. Mind he's not too set in his ways for you, Rachel.

RACHEL

Don't you worry about that. If he is, I'll un-settle them for him quick enough.

MRS JONES

Hmm .... I wish you more luck than I had with our Will. He's a boy and a half, he is - and his old dad's a darn sight worse than he is. Between the pair of them, I never know if I'm standing on my head or my heels.

RACHEL

(smiling) They weren't half enjoying themselves when I left.

(There is a sudden pounding on the front door and BESSIE bursts into the room USL very much out of breath and with her luscious hat clinging to the back of her head.)

BESSIE

(gasping) Mrs Jones - have you - have you seen our Emlyn?

MRS JONES

No, girl. He hasn't been here.

BESSIE

Well! I went back to the hall for him and Silas Ebenezer said he'd just gone off with your Will and his father.

RACHEL

(sharply) Silas Ebenezer, did you say?

BESSIE	That's right – him.
RACHEL	And he had the cheek to tell me he had to go back for stocktaking.
BESSIE	He was stocktaking all right. Very liquid stock it was, too! He was probably covering up for our Emlyn!
	(Off stage faint sounds of masculine voices can be heard singing 'Bread of Heaven'.)
MRS JONES	Hush a minute .... what's that?
	(All three women rush to the window.)
MRS JONES	That's them now, or I'm a Dutchman!
	(The singing increases in volume.)
BESSIE	Look at that Emlyn conducting them with his tie. I'll tie him! I'll tie him in knots!
MRS JONES	All I can say is it's a good job Will and his father got their arms around each other, or they'd be flat on their faces..... Who's the fourth man? The one behind them?
RACHEL	(aghast) It's Silas! Look at him! He's holding his hat out for a – my gawd! That little boy just threw him a penny!
MRS JONES	(turning from window and rolling up her sleeves) I don't know about you two but I'm ready for action!
	(The singing is obviously right outside the door by now but it peters out.)
RACHEL	Me, too. And if he wants to go back to Ceinwen afterwards, she's welcome to him. Stocktaking indeed! That was the last picture show he takes me to.
BESSIE	(rolling up her sleeves and putting her hat on the table DR) Action! I'll paralyse him with action!
	(There is a tentative knock on the door.)
MRS JONES	(softly) Ready, girls?
	(There is another knock on the door. BESSIE, MRS JONES and RACHEL take up strategic posi-

SHERRY IN THE TRIFLE

tions by the door.)

RACHEL   Oh, yes, we're ready!

MRS JONES   (calling out invitingly) Come on in, boys, come on in! We've got a lovely surprise for you!

(Cautiously the door opens and four rather tired looking hats are thrown in, following one another in rapid succession .... as the curtain falls.)

THE END

9/125